D1546711

CONTEMPORARY ART SONGS

28 Songs by American and British Composers

ED-2819

ISBN 978-0-7935-4548-3

G. SCHIRMER, Inc.

DISTRIBUTED BY

HAL•LEONARD
CORPORATION

7777 W. BLUEMOUND RD. P.O. BOX 13819 MILWAUKEE, WI 53213

CONTENTS

Must the winter come so soon?

from the opera "Vanessa"

Gian Carlo Menotti

Samuel Barber

* ⌐¬ = triplet throughout

46679c

and_from his house of brit-tle bark_ hoots_ the fro - zen owl.

Must the win-ter come so soon?

Here_____ in this for - est nei-ther dawn nor sun - set

marks the pas-sing of the days.

It is a long win-ter here.

Must the win-ter come so soon?

46679

Song of Devotion

Text adapted from Philippians I:3-11

John Ness Beck

And this I pray, that your love may a - bound yet more and more in

knowl-edge and in all judg-ment, that ye may ap-prove things that are ex-cel-lent, that

ye may be sin-cere,_be-ing filled with the fruits of right-eous-ness_ un-to the

glo-ry and praise of God. _

I thank my God ____ on ev'ry re-
mem - brance of you, al-ways ____ in ev-'ry prayer of mine for
you with joy; ____ I have you in my ____ heart, ____
I have you in my heart. ____

For Jennie

I
Extinguish my eyes...

Rainer Maria Rilke
English translation by
Jessie Lemont*

Leonard Bernstein

my heart,   my   brain will take   fire   of   you,___

As   flax   takes   fire from a   brand!___

And   flame_ will   sweep___   in a   flood:___

II
When my soul touches yours...

Rainer Maria Rilke
English translation by
Jessie Lemont *

Leonard Bernstein

When my soul touch-es yours a great chord sings:

How can I tune it then to oth-er things? Oh,

_ if some spot in dark-ness could be found That does not vi-brate when your

pp legatissimo (mezza voce)

depths sound! But ev-'ry-thing that touch-es

you and me welds us as played strings sound one mel-o-dy.

Where, where is the in-stru-ment whence the sounds

Heavenly Grass

Tennessee Williams

Paul Bowles

feet took a walk In heav - en-ly grass. All night while the lone - some

stars rolled past, Then my feet come down to walk on earth And my

moth - er cried When she give me birth.

"When I bring to you colour'd toys

Rabindranàth Tagore

John Alden Carpenter
June-September, 1913

col-ours on clouds, _____ on wa - ter, ___ and why

flow'rs are paint-ed in tints: when I give colour'd toys to

you, _____ my child. _____

When I sing to make you dance, I tru-ly know why there is

mu - sic in leaves,_____ and why waves send their cho-rus of

voi - ces to the heart of the lis-ten-ing earth:_____

When I sing to make you dance.

When I bring sweet things to your greedy hands, I

know why there is hon-ey in the cup of the flower and why fruits are secretly

Segador
The Reaper

Carlos Pellicer*
English version by Willis Wager

Carlos Chávez
1938

* Words printed by special permission

Meno mosso ♩ = 58.

Su sombra a - lar - ga - ba la tar - de. En los
His grow-ing shad-ow length-ens the eve - ning. 'Neath his

Poco più ♩ = 63

o - jos___ tra - í - a un lu - ce - ro que a
eye-lids___ he bears a glint of star-light which will

ve - ces brin - ca - ba por to - do el pai - sa - je.___
some-times go danc-ing all o - ver the land - scape.___

Poco più ♩ = 76

Vocalise

WILBUR CHENOWETH

Vocalize throughout with "Ah"

46679

International Copyright Secured

For Marion Williams

Christmas at the Cloisters

William Hoffman

John Corigliano

Orchestra material on rental.

46679

The straw child, The wood child,_____ The ho-ly doll,_ Lives_ a-gain. Praise Him! The in-no-cent, The pen-i-tent, Re-deem-er and mar-ty,_ Cries_ a-gain._____ Praise_____

The up-town Christ,
The Hud-son guest,
The In-wood babe,
Smiles a-gain. Praise Him!
The new one,
The third one,

For W. H.

The Unicorn

William Hoffman

John Corigliano

Now, now as buds grow And snow melts in parks,

And black be - fore, far a - way, The trees verge

pur - ple on the Pal - i - sades, Pale boy, Make clear

Orchestra material on rental.

46679

grass-starved cit - y Grows weeds in the street, Quick boy,

come to me cold!___ Let our swell and sweet bend_ Warm___ these_

woods . . .___ Lest Spring catch you

three nights sad, When fog___ ob - scures the bridge And stars___

shim-mer in the arc lamp haze;_____ Lest tu - bers and

ten - drils and red oak, Yel - low stream - 'ers, And the smell of

mud and riv - er Catch the u - - - ni - corn

Who thinks love,_____ like vi - sion, Pro - ceeds from *his*_____ eyes.

Sound the Flute!

William Blake

Celius Dougherty

46679

Lit-tle Boy, Full of Joy; Lit-tle Girl, Sweet and small;

Cock does crow, So do you; Mer-ry voice, In - fant noise;

Mer-ri-ly, Mer-ri-ly, Mer - ri -ly, To wel - come in the Year.

To John Hanks

Peggy Mitchell

James Stephens*

John Duke

*Used by permission.

46679

So grew she, As eas - i - ly!

Or as the rose, That takes no care, Will o-pen out, on sun-ny air

Bloom aft-er bloom, Fair aft-er fair;

Just so   did she   As care - less - ly!

She____ is our tor-ment with-out end!

She is our en - e-my, our friend!____ Our joy,   our woe!

To the Queen of Heaven

Poem Old English
(16th Century.)

Music by
THOMAS F. DUNHILL

hea-ven, bless'd may thou be, For God - ës Son born He was of thee,

A choral version of this song, for S.A.T.B., is published as Octavo No. 8327

46679

For to make us free,＿＿＿＿ Glo -

- ri - a Ti - bi Dom - in - e.＿＿＿＿

Jes - u, God's

When I was one-and-twenty.

Poem from "A SHROPSHIRE LAD."
A. E. HOUSMAN.
Published by Grant Richards Ltd.
By permission.

Music by
C. ARMSTRONG GIBBS.

I was one-and-twen-ty I heard him say a-

-gain, 'The heart out of the bo - som Was

nev - er given in vain; 'Tis

paid with sighs a plen - ty And sold for end-less

rue.' And I am two-and-

-twen - ty, And oh, 'tis true, 'tis true.

To Bill Wendlandt

An Immorality

Ezra Pound*

Lee Hoiby

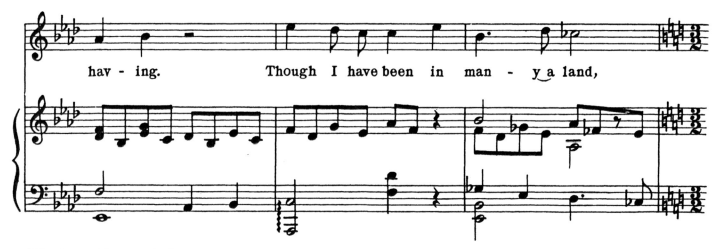

*Words used by permission

46679

There is naught else in liv - ing.

And I ____ would rath - er have my

sweet, ____ Though rose - leaves die of

August 8, 1952
Peterborough, N. H.

Down Harley Street

Benjamin Musser *

Charles Kingsford

*Words used by exclusive permission.

46679

he should whis-tle down Har - ley Street; What right has he to keep on whis-tling When

life is so rot-ten that once was sweet? His face shines red as a rus- set ap-ple, His

walk has a swing, there's gold in his hair. Har-ley Street waits for his jol - ly whis-tle, Since

life is a prop-er- ly rot-ten af-fair.

*Melody of final two measures may be whistled.

Lullaby

from the Musical Drama "The Consul"

Words and Music by
Gian-Carlo Menotti
Piano reduction by
Thomas Schippers

46679

Ba - by won't know. His laugh-ter is blind. Sleep, my love, for sleep is kind.

Sleep is kind when sleep is young. Sleep for me, sleep for me.

I shall build for you planes and boats. I shall catch for you

crick-et and bee. Let the old ones watch your sleep. On-ly death will

watch the old. Sleep, sleep,_____ sleep, sleep, sleep,

sleep._____ Sleep, sleep._____

The Dove Song
Milly's Aria
from: The Wings of the Dove

Ethan Ayer

Douglas Moore

46679

And lov - ers, as they will, Hold hands a -

bove, I'd fol - low them un - til The

dark - ness hides the hill _____ Were I a

cresc. f mf

mf

dove,＿＿＿＿＿＿＿ were I a dove.＿＿＿＿

But all＿＿＿＿＿ fri -

vol - i - ty＿＿＿ That there＿＿＿ is go - ing to＿be＿

dove,_____ were I_____ a dove._____

rit. *a tempo*

Were I a dove the snow Of

win - ter would not blow That kept me down be-low, When up a-bove A

Stopping by Woods on a Snowy Evening

Robert Frost*

Paul Sargent

*From "Collected Poems of Robert Frost". Used by permission of the publishers, Henry Holt & Co., Inc.

watch his woods fill up with snow._____ My

with more movement

lit - tle horse must think it queer To stop with-out a farm-house

near_____ Be - tween the woods and fro - zen lake The

keep, And miles to go _____ be - fore I

sleep, And miles _____ to go be - fore I

sleep. _____

Holiday Song

Genevieve Taggard*

William Schuman
Arranged by the composer

When was it ev - er a
waste of time to climb__ hills? When was it ev - er a
use - less thing to sing the song of a long jol - ly day in the sun?

*Words printed by exclusive permission

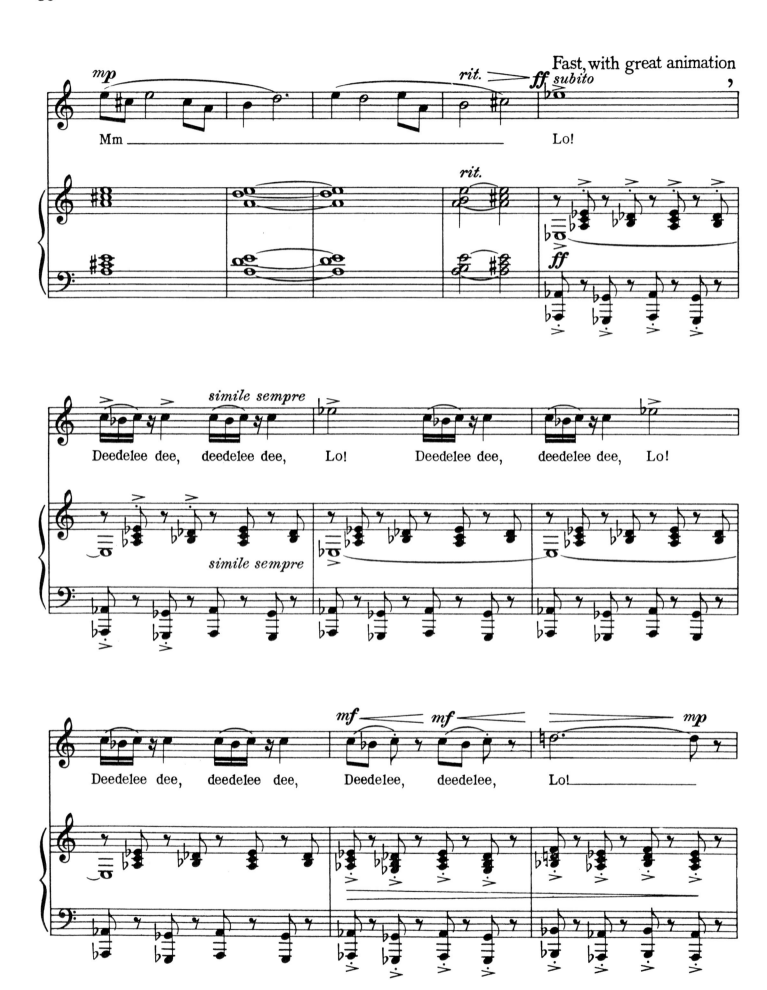

Tempo I moderato ♩ circa 100

When was it ev - er a waste of time to climb__ hills _____

__ or to sing on our hills the song of a long jol-ly day in the sun?

Tempo I ♩. circa 100 *(no slower)*

All of us, ev - 'ry-one,

fff with energy and precision

ev - 'ry - one, all of us, all of us, ev - 'ry - one, ev - 'ry - one,

stacc. sempre

all of us, ev - 'ry-one of us, ev - 'ry- one of us,

ev - 'ry-one of us, ev - 'ry-one of us, all of us,

ev - 'ry - one, all of us, ev - 'ry - one, all of us,

ev - 'ry - one of us has some-thing to sing a - bout,__ has

some-thing to sing a - bout, to sing and shout, to sing and

Tempo II circa 160

shout, shout! Lo!

Deedelee dee, deedelee dee,

Lo! Deedelee dee, deedelee dee, deedelee dee.

Dee - a, dee - a, dee - a, dee - a, Lo! _____

New Rochelle, N.Y.
May 26, 1942
Arranged for solo
voice May, 1946

To Ralph Vaughan Williams.

EASTER CAROL.

CHRISTINA ROSSETTI.
By kind permission of Messrs. Macmillan & Co

MARTIN SHAW.

Spring_____ bursts to - day, For Christ is_ ris'n and all_____ the earth's at play. Flash forth, thou Sun,

The rain is ov-er and gone,_____ its work_____ is done. Win - ter is past, Sweet Spring is come at last,_____ is come at last. Bud, Fig and Vine, Bud,

Ol - ive, fat with fruit and oil_____ and wine

poco rit.　　　　*mp espressivo*

Break forth this morn in ro - ses, thou but

yes - ter - day a Thorn. Up - lift thy head O pure white

Li - ly through__ the win - - ter dead.

poco rit.　　　　a tempo

To URSULA GREVILLE

A sight in Camp

Poem by
WALT WHITMAN

Music by
DOM THOMAS SYMONS

46679

Three forms I see on stretchers ly-ing, brought out there un-tend-ed

ly - ing, O - ver each the blan - ket spread,

am - ple brown-ish wool-len blan-ket, Grey and hea-vy blan-ket,

fold - ing, cov-er-ing all. Cu - ri-ous I halt and si-lent stand,

I love all graceful things

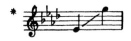

Poem by
KATHLEEN BOLAND
By permission

Music by
ERIC H. THIMAN

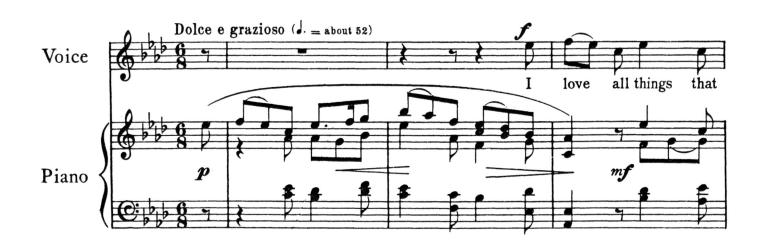

* Available in Key G. Curwen Edition 71977

46679

English Usage

or

"Strike till the iron is hot"

Lyman Abbott

Marianne Moore

Virgil Thomson

Words used by permission of Viking Press.

jus-ti - fied)   or   "friv-o-lous fool"   (how-ev-er   suit - a-ble).

I've   es-caped, eh?   am still   trapped by   these   word

— dis - eas - es.   No   paus - es—   the

phra - ses   lack   lyr - ic   force;_____   sound   ca - pric - like

46679

At-tic Af-ric - Al-ca-ic   or freak cal-i-co Greek._   (Not   verse of course)

I'm   sure of this.

Noth-ing mun-dane is di - vine;___   Noth-ing   di-vine is mun - dane.

rall. molto

cresc. poco a poco

Peterborough, N. H., August 8, 1963

The Tiger

William Blake

Virgil Thomson

46679

Could frame __ thy __ fear - ful __ sym-me-try?

In what dis-tant deeps or skies Burnt the

fire __ of thine eyes? On what wings dare he __ as - pire? What the

hand dare seize the fire?

46679

To Grace Lovat Fraser.

The Inn.

Poem by
HILAIRE BELLOC.

By permission of the publishers
GERALD DUCKWORTH & Co., Ltd.

Music by
FRANCIS TOYE.

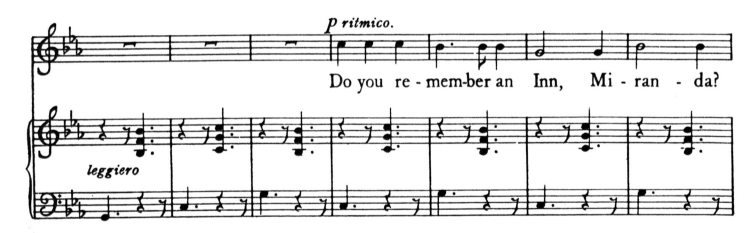

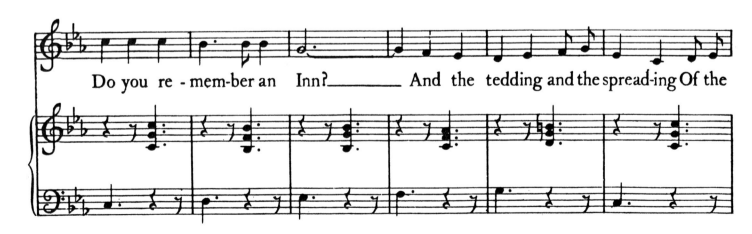

straw for a bed-ding, And the fleas___ that tease in the High Py - re -

nees, And the wine_____ that tast-ed_____ of the tar?_____

un poco piu forte

And the cheers and the jeer._____ of the young mu-le -

sempre p

teers_____ (Un-der the vine of the dark ver - an - dah)

un pochino più forte.

Do you re-mem-ber an Inn, Mi - ran - da? Do you re-mem-ber an

Inn?

senza rall.

pp

cres - cen - do - - - - -

mf *sempre cresc. - - - - - f* senza rall.

Hugh's Song of the Road.

Words by
HAROLD CHILD.

Music by
R. VAUGHAN WILLIAMS.

Più lento.   a tempo.

by,____ Do they call you in the noon-day when the blood runs high?____

Camp-fires, camp-fires, now the west is glow-ing,

Send their rud-dy smoke up to greet the bright'ning moon. Not a roof to shield your head from

free winds blow-ing, Not a wall to deaden the wa-ter's lul-ling tune!

Cook-ing round the camp-fires, bu - sy sounds and cheery, Meat and drink for bel-ly and the

clinging turf for side. Oh! to stretch your length when your back and bones are wea-ry,

Dew-y sleep on clos-ing eyes from heaven's o - pen wide.

Camp-fires, camp-fires, rud-dy in the gloom, Do they

mer - ry stars are peep - ing, Ah! _____ to stretch out emp - ty

arms and fold a wan-der-ing air! _____

All the scent - ed night breathes of beau-ty and of lov-ing;

Tempo I

Heart - beats — swer with a bro - -ken cry,_ Call - ing for a

bride with cour-age to go rov - ing, To dare the world for love beneath the o - - - - pen sky.

Heart-beats, heart-beats, throbbing for the bride; Do they call you in the midnight to a strong man's side?

To Michael Strater

Everyone Sang

Siegfried Sassoon

Howard Wells

light _____ As pris - oned birds

must find in free - dom _____ Wing - ing

wild - ly a - cross the white or - chards _____

and dark green fields _____

And beau - - ty came like the set - ting

sun. _____ My heart was shak-en with

tears And hor - ror drift-ed a - way.

O but